DOGS THROUGHOUT HISTORY™

The Story of the Dalmatian

Jennifer Quasha

The Rosen Publishing Group's
PowerKids Press™
New York

For Weemer

Published in 2000 by The Rosen Publishing Group, Inc.
29 East 21st Street, New York, NY 10010

First Edition

Book design: Danielle Primiceri

Photo credits: Cover © Barbara Wright/Animals Animals; p. 4 © Noble Stock/International Stock; p. 7 © Peter Harholdt/Superstock; p.8 © Reed/Williams/Animals Animals; p. 11 © Archive Photos; pp. 12, 20 © Mary Evans Collection, Inc.; p.15 © Robert Pearcy/Animals Animals; p. 16 © CORBIS/Bettmann; p. 19 © Disney/Everett Collection, Inc.

Quasha, Jennifer.
      The story of the Dalmatian / by Jennifer Quasha.
            p.   cm.—(Dogs throughout history)
      Includes index
      Summary: Relates the history of the Dalmatian from the 1600s to the present, describing their roles as coach dogs, firehouse dogs, and their work for the American military in World War II.
      ISBN 0-8239-5515-X (lib. bdg.)
      1. Dalmatian dog—History—Juvenile literature. 2. Dalmatian dog—Juvenile literature. [1. Dalmatian dog. 2. Dogs.] I. Title. II. Series.
SF429.D3Q37 1998
636.72—dc21   98-49409
                                                                              CIP
                                                                              AC

Manufactured in the United States of America

Contents

Where Do Dalmatians Come From?

Everybody knows a Dalmatian when they see one. This is because of the dog's beautiful spotted **coat**. Dalmatians are very popular and live all over the world. Where did these spotted dogs come from? No one actually knows. There are a lot of different ideas about the **origin** of the Dalmatian. Some people believe that Dalmatians came from India and that Indian **merchants** brought Dalmatians to ancient Greece. Other people believe these dogs came from an area in Europe called Dalmatia. Ancient artwork shows that although their history is unclear, these spotted dogs have existed throughout Europe for a very long time.

◀ *Dalmatians are known for their spots.*

Early Dalmatians in Art

The first known drawing of a dog that looks like a Dalmatian shows a spotted dog running beside a chariot. This drawing probably dates back to Egypt or Babylon. One of the first paintings of an early Dalmatian is a **fresco** in Athens, Greece. A fresco is a painting done on a wall made of **plaster**. The fresco from 1700 B.C. shows white dogs with black and brown spots hunting a boar. Another fresco in a church in Florence, Italy, is of a wolf biting a lamb. Spotted dogs that look like Dalmatians are attacking the wolf to try to protect the lamb.

Can you find the spotted dog in this tapestry from the 1700s? ▶

Austria

Slovania

Croatia

Bosnia

Serbia

Italy

A Place Called Dalmatia

No one really knows how Dalmatians got their name. Some people think the name came from a place called Dalmatia since Dalmatia and Dalmatian sound so much alike. Dalmatia is an area of Croatia, a country in Europe. Not all Dalmatian lovers agree that this is true, though. There is no real **evidence** that Dalmatians came from Dalmatia. It is known that they were brought there in the 1930s by a wealthy Englishman named Mr. Bozo Banac. His spotted dogs lived there for a while but later died out. Today there are no Dalmatians living in Dalmatia.

◀ *Some people believe that Dalmatians came from Dalmatia, an area in Croatia.*

The Dalmatian's Spotted Coat

Some people believe the Dalmatian got its name because of its spotted coat. In the 1600s European priests, bishops, and some **monarchs** wore white tunics, or coats. This coat was called a **dalmatic**. Dalmatics were made of white wool and often had collars made from the white fur of an animal called an ermine. An ermine's tail has a black tip, and the dark tips showed up clearly against the white cloth. These black spots on the white background of the priests' coats were similar to the Dalmatian's coat.

The man kneeling in this picture is wearing a dalmatic. Can you see why Dalmatians might have been named after this robe? ▶

Dalmatians as Coach Dogs

Throughout their history, Dalmatians have been very helpful to people. In the 1600s in England, wealthy people who owned carriages used Dalmatians as coach dogs. Having a Dalmatian as a coach dog was a **symbol** of wealth. Usually each coach or carriage had only one Dalmatian. A coach dog would run alongside the horse and carriage to protect it from robbers. When the passengers got out of the carriage, the Dalmatian would continue to stand guard by the coach. Soon people in America wanted coach dogs, too. In fact, George Washington, the first president of the United States, bought a Dalmatian on August 12, 1787. Dalmatians were on their way to becoming some of the most popular dogs in America.

◄ *A Dalmation coach dog runs alongside an English carriage.*

Dalmatians in the Firehouse

Dalmatians were also helpful to firefighters. In England during the 1600s, fire trucks were actually horse-drawn carriages carrying tanks filled with water. The people who fought fires were members of fire **brigades**. A brigade is a group of people working together for the same cause. In this case, the cause was putting out fires. Dalmatians helped by running ahead of the fire brigades and barking to clear the way. Fire fighters soon fell in love with these special dogs. Even when the fire truck replaced the carriage in the late 1800s, Dalmatians stayed in the firehouse to help their firefighter friends.

Dalmatians still live in firehouses today. ▶

Dalmatians Help in War

During World War II, which was fought between 1939 and 1945, American soldiers used Dalmatians to help in the fight against their enemies. These **heroic** dogs were taught how to carry messages from one person to another and to bring **Red Cross** supply kits to soldiers. They were also good at rescuing soldiers when they were buried under rocks, dirt, and **debris**. The Dalmatians would use their powerful sense of smell to locate trapped soldiers and then dig the soldiers out using their paws. Dalmatians were also good at guarding soldiers' property. These brave Dalmatians saved many lives with their wartime work.

◄ *This helpful Dalmatian works with someone from the Red Cross.*

101 Dalmatians

In 1956, author Dodie Smith wrote a book called *One Hundred and One Dalmatians*. The story is about two Dalmatians, Pongo and Perdita, whose 99 puppies are stolen by an evil lady named Cruella De Vil. Cruella De Vil wants to make a spotted coat using the puppies' fur. With the help of their human friends, Roger and Anita, Pongo and Perdita are able to save their puppies from Cruella De Vil. All 101 Dalmatians end up happy and safe. People loved this wonderful story so much that two movies were made from it. Both versions of the movie *101 Dalmatians* helped Dalmatians become one of the most loved dogs throughout the world.

These cute cartoon puppies from the movie made lots of people want to own Dalmatians. ▶

Dalmatians in the Circus

Dalmatians don't only star in movies, they also star in the circus. Many Dalmatians work with circus **troupes** throughout the United States. Dalmatians are smart, and they learn circus tricks quickly. Some Dalmatians learn to climb ladders. Others wear clown suits and roll around in large barrels. They can jump over sticks and walk on tightropes. These amazing dogs are wonderful to watch. They are not only adorable and smart, they are very talented, too.

◄ *Dalmatians are great circus dogs because they are smart and learn tricks easily. The Dalmatian in this picture waits for his turn to perform.*

Dalmatians Today

Dalmatians are one of the most unique-looking dogs today. These medium-sized dogs are strong, sleek, and handsome. Although they are born all white, Dalmatian puppies soon develop dark spots on their coats. Their cute spots are only one of the reasons Dalmatians are so special. These dogs are wonderful with children and adults. They are smart and **sensitive**, and love to spend time with their owners. Their energy and spirit have made them popular around the world. Dalmatians have been helpful dogs throughout their long history and continue to be wonderful companions for people today.

Web Sites:

http://www.puppyshop.com/caninebreeds/
  dalmatian.htm
http://www.dalmatians.com/

Glossary

brigade (brih-GAYD) A group of people organized to work together.

coat (COHT) An animal's fur.

dalmatic (dahl-MAH-tik) A white and black coat worn by priests.

debris (duh-BREE) Pieces of wood, glass, stone, and other materials left after a disaster.

evidence (EH-vih-dints) Facts that prove something.

fresco (FRESS-coh) A watercolor painting done on plaster.

heroic (hih-ROH-ik) Brave or courageous.

merchant (MUR-chint) Someone who sells things.

monarchs (MAH-narks) Kings and queens.

origin (OR-ih-gin) Where something comes from.

plaster (PLAS-tur) A mixture of lime, sand, and water that hardens as it dries.

Red Cross (REHD CROSS) A group that helps people in trouble all around the world.

sensitive (SEN-sih-tihv) Being very aware of what is going on around you.

symbol (SIM-bul) An object, design, or idea that stands for something else.

troupe (TROOP) A group of people that performs.

Index